- Successful Dating -

No More Frogs
CANCER

21 June – 22 July

by
Cathrine Dahl

CONTENTS

- Successful Dating -
No More Frogs

by Cathrine Dahl

No More Frogs - Successful Dating is your one-stop dating guide. No unnecessary blah-blah. The information is right here, at your fingertips.

This guide can be used in several ways. It's a handy tool when you want to prepare yourself a little. It can give you an advantage when going on a date or getting to know someone you've just met - or even someone you've known for a while.

Although this guide can help you angle your approach, remember to be true to yourself. Have fun, be wise, follow your heart - and keep your feet on the ground!

- Cathrine Dahl

Preface:
A few words about compatibility, and why compatibility guides can give you the wrong idea.

So you've met this Gemini you really, really like, but you're a Scorpio, and the compatibility guides say you're a lousy match. Guess what? That's rubbish!

Some compatibility guides offer a very simplistic approach, claiming that your best matches are the star signs within the same element as you:

Fire: Aries, Leo and Sagittarius
Earth: Taurus, Virgo and Capricorn
Air: Gemini, Libra and Aquarius
Water: Cancer, Scorpio and Pisces

Other guides are slightly more specific, declaring that we are compatible with star signs within our astrological polarity.

Yin: Taurus, Virgo, Capricorn, Cancer, Scorpio and Pisces
Yang: Aries, Leo, Sagittarius, Gemini, Libra and Aquarius

Doesn't look too good, does it? The most optimistic approach has removed half of the population from your dating pool. It doesn't make any sense. The true picture is far more promising...

One star sign, two very different personalities

Each of us has a unique astrological thumbprint determined by the sun, the moon and the planets. The most important factors being your ascending star (ascendant), the sun (star sign) and the moon (feelings).

Let's make it simple

Imagine your star sign being a melody. All the other aspects (the unique positioning of the moon and the planets) are sound effects, applied by a producer with a mixer.

The combination of rhythm, depth and base creates your unique sound. Another person with the same star sign will get his own sound mix and end up with a different beat.

Your personal melody can create wonderful harmonies with star signs you're not supposed to get on with – and nothing but noise with signs that are meant to be matches. You won't find out until you get to know each other.

Let's get to know your date...

THE MALE

YOUR DATE: CANCER
21 June–22 July

The Essence of him

Masculine – elegant – stylish – reserved – polite – attentive – patient – sympathetic – caring – compassionate – sensitive – moody – has strong bonds with friends and family – sensible – goal-oriented – ambitious – has a good memory – intensely feeling – insecure – kind – considerate – empathetic – jealous – big-hearted – romantic – a dreamer – a good listener

...and remember: Although he is strong and masculine, the Cancer man needs reassurance. Never leave him wondering about your feelings or your intentions. That'll make him insecure and miserable.

Blind Date – speedy essentials

Who's waiting for you?

Stylish and relaxed, with a broad smile ... there's no doubt about it, this is a manly man. His masculinity shines through his personality, not through a tight-fitting t-shirt. He is naturally gallant, polite and attentive: it's as though he was born to be a gentleman. You'll find no macho tendencies, no raucous laughter or silly jokes, no intense and analysing stares. He will do his best to make you feel relaxed and at ease in his company. However, don't expect too much from his outfit. This is no fashion icon. He prefers to keep it casual.

Emergency fixes for embarrassing pauses

Don't worry about pauses. As soon as he has eased into the role, he will gladly guide you through conversation and ask questions to help you loosen up a bit. Pauses will usually only occur if the two of you don't have anything in common. Be positive and entertaining. He will notice the vibes, and everything will flow freely and naturally.

Your place or mine?

He's passionate and romantic, but not at the expense of his politeness and gallantry. He will rarely have sex with a woman on the first date. There are several reasons for this: first, feelings become involved in everything he does, including sex. He doesn't want to waste his sensitivity on a one-night stand. Another reason is that in order to fully appreciate the sensuality, he needs to know the woman he is making love to.

Checklist, before you dash out to meet him:

Look neat and tidy
(hint: no chipped nail varnish)
Don't have work or appointments later
(hint: be relaxed; no stress)
Leave your apartment clean and organised
(hint: in case he joins you home)
Bring a small casual gift (e.g. homemade candy)
(hint: show you made an effort)
Be brushed up on books, movies and TV shows
(hint: be interesting)

Tip: Never act insensitive around this guy. Don't make fun of him, even if you're just pulling his leg. He will take these statements to heart. A silly comment could actually ruin the entire evening.

CHAPTER 1

PREPARE YOURSELF

Catch his eye, capture his attention
Top 10 attention grabbers

1. Spark his interest with a playful look.
2. Be sparkling and outgoing.
3. Make sure your personality radiates positivity.
4. Wear an outfit that emphasises your femininity – but nothing vulgar.
5. Wear a bright smile.
6. Show a genuine interest in him and his world.
7. Admire him, but make it intelligent and specific – not just a general 'wow'.
8. Be very neat: your eyebrows, nails and make-up should be flawless.
9. Have a good sense of humour. It will be a big plus if you can praise yourself with humour.
10. Be intelligent and ask for his opinion.

The SHE. The woman!

It takes a special woman to hold onto this man. It's not enough to be feminine and positive – she must also be strong enough to handle his moodiness. She must be flexible in her ways. She must be loyal. She must strive to fill the days with harmony. Charming, humble, supportive and smart ... it's no easy task, but it's worth it.

The Essence of her
Feminine – sparkling – compassionate – patient – flexible – harmonious –intelligent – warm – caring – down-to-earth – has a positive attitude – radiates joy and happiness – allows her man to be a man – entertaining – inspiring – supportive – pays attentive to detail – trustworthy – loyal – outgoing and charming –reassuring –gentle – humorous – shows her feelings

Cancer arousal meter
From 0 to 100... In three hours or more. Throwing yourself at him will seldom spark his erotic interest. Give him time to loosen up.

Remember: Be true to yourself

It doesn't matter if he is the most stunning guy you've ever met – if you don't match, you don't match. You may be able to put on a show for a while to hold his attention, but what's the point? We can't please everybody. We all have different needs, dreams, tastes and preferences. There's no such thing as a one-size-fits-all lover. Be yourself, and be true to who you are – always!

Very important: Show interest and admiration for him, but allow him to take the initiative. Never throw yourself at him.

CHAPTER 2

THE FIRST DATE

Getting your foot in the door
The basics

Support. This guy may be looking for a woman to fill the gaps in his life – whatever he feels he's missing. He's seeking someone supportive and loyal who he can trust.

Good vibes. She must also be able to add sunshine and harmony to his life. It's important that you radiate optimism, enthusiasm and positivity. A woman who helps him relax and feel good will always have an advantage.

Sharp, smart and sensitive. Inner beauty and intellectual qualities mean a lot to him. Inspire him with intelligent questions. Show him that you have an independent mind.

No mysteries. Avoid anything that will make him feel insecure about you. Evasiveness and mystery won't work with this guy. Be genuine and be direct – without being blunt or aggressive. Don't play hard to get. If you want to see him again, let him know – but do it in a feminine way.

Ease into him. Never make him feel cornered. Finding the right balance is a challenge. But if you really get along, you'll develop a sense of what to do and when. Give him space.

Whatever you do...

- **DON'T** be vulgar in any way.

- **DON'T** criticise his moodiness or sensitivity.

- **DON'T** flirt with other men.

- **DON'T** neglect yourself. Be healthy and look after your body.

- **DON'T** take his attention for granted.

Remember, this man needs reassurance. Don't be afraid to show him how you feel –

- **DON'T** be afraid to speak your mind, but avoid being argumentative.

- **DON'T** focus on the negative components of life. Be positive.

- **DON'T** keep him in the dark about your intentions.

- **DON'T** be sexually aggressive – or aggressive in at all.

- **DON'T** be ignorant. Show him that you have an alert mind.

but be careful and don't be too blunt and direct about it.

Signs you're in - or not

It's not always easy to figure out what's on a Cancer man's mind. He is an expert at protecting his feelings, and he won't reveal anything before he's confident in the relationship. He wants to save you – and himself! – from disappointment. Before this point, he'll probably be a little back and forth, careful not to commit to anything. If you really like him, be patient. Show your charisma and give him time and space to figure things out. When he does, the signals will be clear:

Chances are he will...

- show signs of kindness, like bringing you a little something he thinks you might need or like; it will be something personal
- be attentive and respond to you quickly
- light with happiness up when he sees you
- lose track of time when the two of you are talking
- show interest in your family
- open up about personal matters

Not your type? Making an exit

Let's hope you never find yourself needing to force a break-up with a Cancer. It will be devastating, no matter how down-to-earth you might be. He is sensitive, so any negativity from someone he cares about will upset him. He will usually take the hint quickly. Well, that's not exactly true. If you're being harsh, he will decide you don't live up to his expectations – and he'll think the break-up was his choice. Although he's loyal by nature, he has very little tolerance for ignorant or inconsiderate women.

There are exceptions to this rule, however rare. If you have managed to mesmerise him with your personality, you may need to apply blunter methods. Make sure a break-up is what you want before you take action!

Foolproof exit measures:

There will be no looking back after this. He will completely rule you out of his life. The measures are rough, so be gentle.

- Take him for granted
- Be cold, insensitive and unapproachable
- Insist on making your sex life more exciting by introducing porn and leather toys
- Criticise him for being weak and clingy if he wants to snuggle up
- Let yourself go. Gain weight. Stop visiting the hairdresser
- Introduce vulgarity in to your life: bad language, tacky clothes, etc.

CHAPTER 3

SEX'N STUFF

Seductive moves:
How to get him in the mood:

For a Cancer male, erotic advances must be gentle and subtle. Stuff that may turn on other men can have the opposite effect on him. Aggressiveness and assertiveness will push him away. Instead, try communicating with a smile and a long glance. Follow up with a gentle touch along his arm and over his fingers – and then a gentle kiss...

Preferences and erotic nature

During sex, he is passionate, strong and protective. He cares deeply about his partner's pleasure and enjoys guiding his woman through the mysteries of sex. He will be more than happy to introduce you to new ideas, but he'll always be careful not to push you. Sex with him is never boring and always fulfilling. He has a traditional streak, but he may surprise you by suggesting sex when you least expect it. He's not tied to the bedroom, but he'll never have sex in public places or in situations where you risk being caught. His amazing memory makes him a very exciting and understanding lover. He applies his memory of your previous encounters to make you feel like an erotic princess. He is truly a dream.

Hitting the right buttons

Although every sign has areas that are more sensitive than others, individual sensitivity may vary quite a bit. Don't go body-blind. Honing in on these erogenous zones and forgetting the rest of him is not a good idea. Use his erogenous zones to create sparks while turning him on, and as a passion booster when it gets heated. Watch his body language – including the most obvious of signs! Open your mind to the sensuality of touch and taste.

Key areas
His chest and nipples

Get it on
The Cancer man has two major 'on' buttons. The first are his nipples, which are very sensitive and respond well to soft touches, gentle rubbing, smooth lips or a playful tongue. The second is kissing, which appeals to his sensitivity and emotions – and this can also get him going.

Arouse him
Bring out your own sensitivity! Kiss him super gently, and take things from there. Never rush things. Let the feelings develop naturally. Caress him carefully and press yourself gently against his. Allow the kiss to become something that involves his entire body.

Surprise him

Take the initiative to be close to him. When you're out in public, press yourself against him – but only if the situation allows it; avoid tacky or clingy behaviour. A sensitive backrub when he least expects it can quickly turn into something more erotic, provided you are patient, gentle and sensitive about it.

Spice it up

The Cancer man is receptive to gentle touches. Keep this in mind, and have a play with oils, creams ... and maybe a little ice cream around his nipples.

Remember: Reassurance is important to him. Communicate your pleasure through voice and body.

His expectations

Sensual guidance. He expects his partner to encourage him in bed, but in a subtle and sensual way.

No constructive criticism! His woman must be careful not to criticise him in bed. That will have the same effect as throwing a bucket of ice in his face.

Seize the moment and enjoy. Take things slow. Enjoy the journey, and don't rush to reach climax.

Connect through intimacy. A long foreplay is very important to him. It feels good physically and enables him to connect emotionally.

Not just a physical thing. He experience erotic feelings on many levels. Everything is part of the bigger picture.

The tender touch. His partner must be sensitive and good at expressing her feelings through gentle touch, whispers and kissing.

Soft sensuality. Feminine underwear can be a great turn-on for this man – he likes anything that emphasises a woman's curves and femininity.

Your sensual preferences
Quiz yourself and find out whether this man is for you.

Where on the scale are you?
1 = Don't agree | 3 = Sure | 5 = Agree!

1. Kissing is an important part of sex and sensuality.
One a scale for 1 to 5, you are: 1 - 2 - 3- 4 - 5

2. Quiet intimacy can be more arousing than intense passion.
One a scale for 1 to 5, you are: 1 - 2 - 3- 4 - 5

3. The enjoyment of sex is not limited to physicality.
One a scale for 1 to 5, you are: 1 - 2 - 3- 4 - 5

4. Sensuality is a great way to express feelings.
One a scale for 1 to 5, you are: 1 - 2 - 3- 4 - 5

Score 15–20: Oh, wow ... this is the stuff that sensual dreams are made of.
10 - 14: You share some important values and are able to inspire each other. It's a good start!
5 - 9: This is possible, but it'll take effort and mutual understanding to make it work.
1 - 4: You'll need to communicate and make some adjustments to achieve a fulfilling sex life.

CHAPTER 4

GENERAL STUFF

The big picture

Keep in mind that the characteristics of a Cancer may vary quite a bit depending on where within the sign he was born, as well as a wide range of additional astrological factors. But for now, let's stick to the basics. Just remember: don't jump to conclusions as soon as you meet him. Give him room to shine. Get to know the man behind the sign.

His personality: Pros and cons

Pros	Cons
• Romantic	• Moody
• Sensitive	• Jealous
• Masculine	• Self-obsessed
• Assertive	• Guarded and reserved
• Kind	• Insecure
• Intelligent	• Afraid of romantic failure
• A good listener	• Easily hurt
• Big-hearted	• Overly sensitive
• Patient	• Demanding
• Sympathetic	• Judgmental
• Ambitious	• Sulky
• Attentive	• Withdrawn
• Has a good memory	• Indecisive
• A loyal friend	• Easily influenced

Tip: How to show romantic interest

This is a perceptive guy – and that's why you have to be careful not to give him the wrong idea. Make sure that whatever you do has a personal touch and shows that you've been thinking about him: a special gift; a show or concert. Be thoughtful and make it personal.

Romantic Vibes

Mr Cancer:
The sensitive and masculine partner

The essence

Popular guy. It doesn't take much for him to become interested in someone. Since he's committed to finding the woman of his dreams, he may date quite a few.

Committed. It may take a while, but when he does commit to a relationship, he will very seldom stray. The essence of his world is love – but he's particular, and his partner must live up to his physical and mental expectations.

Loyal. He is very loyal to his old friends. If a new date doesn't approve of them, he will choose his friends over her – no matter how fascinated he might be.

No party-animal. The right woman doesn't have to worry. This man won't spend the whole night partying with the guys. In fact, he won't take a break from her very often. She is his source of love and inspiration, so why risk upsetting her?

Cherish the love. He must feel loved in order to thrive in a relationship. Fights, irritability, criticism, and sarcastic remarks will make him rethink the relationship no matter how strong his feelings might be.

The Sensitive and loving Alpha Male. Although he is sensitive, warm and caring, he still sees himself as The Man who makes the decisions.

Tip: How to show erotic interest

His sensuality is linked to his feelings. If you have reached a certain level of emotional connection with him, try gentle kisses.

Erotic Vibrations

Mr Cancer:
The romantic and strong lover

The essence

Seductive magic. He has the ability of seducing you without you even noticing. He is so subtle and sensitive, that you'll melt in his arms without thinking about it.

The fire within. He is one of the most romantic men in the zodiac – both in bed and out. However, sex with him is no sweet and innocent encounter. The right woman will bring out the masculinity and passion in him, and the sex will be intense with and beautiful.

True essence of sensuality. Sex with him is intense and beautiful. There will be no vulgarities. No dirty language. No silly or rude suggestions. He is a true sensual lover.

Master of erotic memory. His memory is excellent, and he'll remember your preferences and build on his knowledge as he goes.

Be sassy, but keep it feminine. He doesn't mind you taking the initiative and being creative, but remember no to overdo it. He wants his woman to be feminine in every aspect of life – including in the bedroom.

An erotic dream. He won't mind teaching you a thing or two in bed, but he will do so very gently: a few whispers in your ear while he guides you.

CHAPTER 5

COMPATIBILITY QUIZ

_____

Are you banging your head against the wall, or does he unleash your positive potential? Do you provoke him or bring out the best in him? Does he make you throw your arms up in exasperation, or do you feel inspired and complete in his company? Are the two of you headed towards doom or dream? Take the test to find out.

Question 1.
Do you always tell your partner about your erotic needs and preferences?

A. Yes, of course.
B. Rarely. My partner is very sensitive. Anything more adventurous than the missionary position would probably offend him.
C. Sometimes, but it depends on my mood ... and how sassy my ideas are!

Question 2.
Do you tend to criticize your partner if there's something you're unhappy with ?

A. Yes. How else am I supposed to get my point through to him?
B. No. If you approach someone with negativity, you'll get negativity in return. I try to be diplomatic.
C. Sometimes, but only if I'm in a bad mood

(cont.)

Question 3.
What comes to mind when you hear the word "sex"?

A. Romance, a sensual setting and pleasure.
B. Joy, passion and satisfaction.
C. Spontaneity, intensity and hot energy.

Question 4.
How do you deal with moodiness?

A. I know it's important to be flexible and understanding, but frequent moodiness drives me nuts.
B. I have very little tolerance for moodiness. It's insensitive to bother other people with your mood swings.
C. There is usually a reason my partner is feeling how he is. If he's low, I try to make him feel better.

Question 5.
Do you find it easy to forgive?

A. No. If someone has hurt me, the anger stays with me for a long time.
B. Forgiveness isn't easy, but I do try my best.
C. If someone asks for forgiveness, it means they have realised that their actions were wrong. The least you can do is forgive them.

Question 6.
How would you react if someone made a joke on your guy's behalf?

A. It'd be okay. We shouldn't take ourselves too seriously.
B. I'd never tolerate that. I always stick up for my guy, whether he's there or not.
C. I would probably hit back with a joke of my own, aimed at her guy.

Question 7.
How do you feel about a guy who takes command when the going gets tough?

A. I really appreciate a strong man I can rely on, providing he doesn't run me over...
B. Pure bliss! He would be my dream man!
C. I've never really been in to macho stuff. Guys like that bore me.

Question 8.
Do you find it easy to express your feelings?

A. It's so important to show how you feel. It removes insecurities and makes?
B. Yes, but sometimes I forget...
C. My guy knows that I love him. There's no need to remind him every day.

Question 9.
How do you feel about kissing?

A. I love it. I could never be in a relationship without kisses. So many feelings are expressed through kissing.
B. No big deal. A kiss is a kiss, right?
C. Kissing is a great way to share closeness and intimacy.

Question 10.
Do you ever tell your partner about previous lovers?

A. Sure. It's part of my past and who I am. Why shouldn't I?
B. Very seldom, and only if I feel I have to.
C. Never, that would be very insensitive.

SCORE	A	B	C
Question 1	10	1	5
Question 2	1	10	5
Question 3	10	5	1
Question 4	5	1	10
Question 5	1	5	10
Question 6	1	10	5
Question 7	5	10	1
Question 8	10	5	1
Question 9	10	1	5
Question 10	1	5	10

75 – 100
Love, sensitivity and harmony have descended upon every area of your life, and it seems to have happened effortlessly and naturally. Your man is masculine and strong – as well as soft and sensitive. There's no either-or; he is everything, and he's the perfect man for you! This relationship promises to be amazing. You know how to handle him when he withdraws into himself. You don't get hurt if he seems distant and stressed, because you know this is his way of dealing with life. Love, respect, understanding and consideration form the foundation of this relationship – which probably will last for quite some time.

51 – 74
Yes, he will probably make your eyes twinkle. And yes, he will sometimes be a challenge! Moodiness is a part of this masculine man, but don't take it personally. He has a lot going on in his mind, and sometimes he just withdraws. Ironically, his sensitivity is exactly the thing that can make him insensitive at times. But you've been looking for a real man, and here he is. He can make your knees turn to jelly, and his romantic streak and sensitivity make him incredibly loveable. Although there might be a few ups and downs, see it through. He's worth it.

26 – 50

There are moments with him that are pure bliss – moments when you're sure you've met the most wonderful man in the world. However, sometimes, when you look into his eyes, you notice a strange seriousness. It's something you can't put your finger on, and he doesn't want to talk about everything – but he expects you to understand. If you don't, he'll be confused. This is part of why it may be difficult to establish complete harmony. Maybe you're too restless for him. Maybe you need more fire and energy in your life. The two of you have different ways of communicating, and sometimes you talk and walk right past each other. It's up to you whether you should keep walking...

10 – 25

How the two of you got together in the first place is a mystery. You were probably attracted to his masculinity and assertiveness. Or maybe it was a classic case of 'opposites attract'? Whatever the spark, it probably won't stay alight very long. His moodiness and sensitivity drive you nuts; meanwhile, he regards you as blunt and distant. This relationship requires a lot of work. It's possible, but is it worth it? Right now, you're probably just annoying each other. Both of you will could find a better match elsewhere. Change course and pursue true happiness and joy.

Thoughts...
Remember, moods can play tricks with your feelings. Don't make rushed decisions. Take a deep breath and think again...

THE FEMALE

YOUR DATE: CANCER
21 June–22 July

The Essence of her

Sensitive – incurably romantic – generous with her time and compassion – loyal– attractive, with a flair for turning every outfit into something stunning – appreciates the beauty in life – dramatic – moody – charming – sensual and seductive – playful – practical – affectionate – kind and considerate

...and remember: She may come across as strong and independent, but she has a sensitive nature and is easily hurt. Mind your words and be careful with criticism. Diplomacy is the key.

Blind Date – speedy essentials

Who's waiting for you?

She would rather not wait for you, but she'll give a bit of slack – provided you have a very good excuse for being late. She is a woman in every sense of the word, and she exudes femininity. You'll see it in her outfit, her make-up, the way she carries herself, her sparkling laugh and the way she looks at you... A Cancer woman won't be shy. Being around men energises her. She is used to male attention, and she expects to be admired. Her standards are high. If you don't meet her expectations, she will be polite and have dinner with you – but that's it. She'll be off and you'll be out.

Emergency fixes for embarrassing pauses.

If you feel a pause coming on, it's your cue to get your act together. She will happily chirp along with a man who fascinates her, but she doesn't like being bored. If the conversation comes to a halt, it's your job to pick it up. Don't try the 'you-look-beautiful-tonight' routine. She already knows – don't patronise her. Focus on ideas or dreams – topics that make her think and connect with you.

Your place or mine?

Either. Ideally, she would like to be whisked away by a prince on a white horse, but this is the 21st century, and she's flexible. She'll probably be open to a fling for one of two reasons: first, if she hopes the guy will turn out to be something worthwhile – or second, if he's stunning and probably good in bed. In either case, he needs to meet her expectations. He must be attractive, manly and attentive.

Checklist, before you dash out to meet her:

Going to a new place? Get directions ahead of time
(hint: don't spend forever trying to find the place)
Be groomed and pay attention to details!
(hint: nails, nose hairs... she'll notice)
Wear something stylish and clean
(hint: don't just throw something on at the last minute)
Be rested and energised
(hint: no yawning!)
Prepare some topics for conversation
(hint: keep her entertained)

Tip: The Cancer woman is generous, compassionate and kind – provided you don't rub her the wrong way. Her tolerance for criticism is very low. Keep it positive.

CHAPTER 1

PREPARE YOURSELF

Catch her eye, capture her attention
Top 10 attention grabbers

1. Be polite: take her coat, open the door etc.
2. Have a confident and relaxed attitude in public.
3. Wear something stylish you stand out.
4. Focus exclusively on her – don't allow for any female competition.
5. Notice something unique about her – even a small detail – and compliment her on it.
6. Be assertive! Show your interest, but without being blunt about it.
7. Portray yourself as masculine and protective.
8. Surprise her: hire a limo for an hour and go sightseeing, or take her on a mini-trip.
9. Add a little extra luxury to a date.
10. Walk up to her with a single flower, and hand it to her even before you speak.

The HE. The man!

Although she's independent and strong, she's looking for a man who can protect her and take care of her. He needs to be someone she can admire and be proud of. Loyalty is very important to her, and her partner must never give her reason to doubt him. She values little gifts and dinner invitations not for the gifts themselves, but for the gestures. They're tokens of love, and she cherishes them.

The Essence of him
Diplomatic – able to handle her various moods – handsome and stylish – generous– attentive – understanding – strong and masculine, without being blunt or macho – romantic – sensitive to the finer things in life –loyal, supportive and faithful –entertaining in social settings – engaging – inclusive

Cancer arousal meter
From 0 to 100... In an hour or a week, depending on how well she knows you – or whether she's really attracted to you. If she's got the hots for you, it may be less than an hour!

Remember: Be true to yourself

It doesn't matter if she is the most stunning girl you've ever met – if you don't match, you don't match. You may be able to put on a show for a while to hold her attention, but what's the point? We can't please everybody. We all have different needs, dreams, tastes and preferences. There's no such thing as a one-size-fits-all lover. Be yourself, and be true to who you are – always!

Very important: Although she can be a great flirt, she's choosy about the men she invites into her life for the longer term. The first impression counts.

CHAPTER 2

THE FIRST DATE

Getting your foot in the door
The basics

No silly remarks. You need to be careful when trying to seduce this woman, as she is one of the most sensitive signs in the zodiac. A stupid remark at the wrong time could ruin the entire evening – and the possibility of a romantic encounter with her!

Don't take anything for granted. She has high standards, but she's not a difficult woman to handle – far from it! She is sympathetic and understanding, and she'll go to great lengths to sort things out with her partner. However, until you capture her heart, you'd better play your cards right!

Be romantic and sensitive. Try an intimate evening in small restaurant with soft music in the background.

Be attentive, both when you're together and when you're not. Notice any changes in her appearance, and after the date, call or text to let her know you're thinking about her.

Be generous. Flowers never go out of fashion with Cancer women. Be generous with your time, as well. Take an extended lunch break to see her, or finish your workday early.

Whatever you do...

- **DON'T** neglect your manners, especially at the table.

- **DON'T** take her for granted. Show appreciation and affection.

- **DON'T** be crude or use bad language.

- **DON'T** try to entertain her with lame jokes or silly stories.

- **DON'T** pinch her bum!

Remember, although you have captured her interest, she'll be quick to turn her back on you if you mess up. Always keep your word!

- **DON'T** tell her the restaurant is 'just fine' if she doesn't like it.

- **DON'T** criticise her friends or family.

- **DON'T** be blunt about your erotic feelings.

- **DON'T** suggest skipping dessert or going for low-calorie items on the menu.

- **DON'T** be sloppy about your appearance.

Be classy, attentive, charming – and someone she can admire. There are no second chances with this girl.

Signs you're in - or not

The Cancer woman enjoys being around men. She flirts and teases – and loves the attention. This is where things can get a little tricky. She may shoot you seductive glances and dazzle you with her charm and laughter, but it doesn't mean she's necessarily attracted to you. Sometimes, male attention is all she's looking for: she expects to get it, and she always does. A man who ignores her will be written off as a nutcase. If she really likes you, there are some signals that may give her away:

Chances are she will...

- buy you a gift – something small but exclusive
- take the initiative to call or text you
- be available on short notice when you ask her out – even during the day
- keep her focus firmly on you when you're out in public
- make hints about the future: an idea about a weekend away together, etc.
- open up and tell you about her preferences – in all areas of her life

Not your type? Making an exit

The Cancer woman has a romantic vision of what a relationship should be. She thinks life would be wonderful if it was like an old-fashioned romance novel. When reality catches up with her, she tries to be practical about it. Although she can be surprisingly realistic, she has a deep longing for love and romance – and she's prepared to endure quite a bit, provided her partner is worth it. If she finds herself in an unhappy relationship, she may prefer to try loads of different things rather than putting her foot down and leave.

If she's not ready to let you go, she will do whatever she can to hold onto you. She will use tears and dramatics. If that doesn't work, get ready for a guilt trip. And her last resort...? Putting up a fight. Breaking up with a female Cancer is no easy task. You'll save yourself a pile of trouble if you can let the initiative come from her.

Foolproof exit measures:

You'll need to make sure you are ready to take these steps, because they'll make you look really bad – and before they work, they will rock the boat more than you thought possible.

- Criticise her when she has made an effort to please you
- Give her a cheap gift picked up from the local petrol station
- Compare her to other women and suggest that she change
- Be quick and selfish in bed
- Suggest having pizza and streaming porn on your date night
- Criticise her opinions and argue over details

CHAPTER 3

SEX'N STUFF

Seductive moves:
How to get her in the mood:

Don't be fooled into thinking you know how to get her going. You may – or you may not. What she needs depends on her mood. Sometimes, she's receptive. Other times, you might as well try to seduce a rock. But no matter how you go about it, remember to be smooth and sensual. If you come on too strong too suddenly, you won't have a chance.

Preferences and erotic nature

She's not an exhibitionist, but she would probably enjoy slowly undressing in front of you. If she does, remember to compliment her body. This will make her even more eager to please you. Sex and romance are two sides of the same coin for a female Cancer, so romantic gestures often arouse her. You'll notice this when you whisper sweet nothings into her ear, gently stroke her hair or give her a tender kiss. These moves can make her knees go weak. But if you carry on caressing her body, you'd better prepare for a long and sensual night.

Hitting the right buttons

Although every sign has areas on the body that are more sensitive than others, individual sensitivity may vary quite a bit. Don't go body-blind. Honing in on these erogenous zones and forgetting the rest of her is not a good idea. Use these areas to create sparks while turning her on, and as a passion-booster when things get heated. Watch her body language – including the most obvious of signs. Open your mind to the sensuality of touch and taste.

Key area
Her chest

Get it on
Take a good look at the female Cancer. Chances are that she's well equipped in the chest area, and this is a good place to focus if you want to bring out the passion in her. This may sound easy, but it's not. Grabbing a boob will probably result in a smack on the head. Your touch needs to be gentle, almost accidental – at least in the beginning...

Arouse her
If you want to arouse her in public, you'll need some finesse. She hates vulgarity, so be subtle. If you're out dancing, let your upper body gently brush against hers. When helping her with her coat, let your hand brush against her breasts. When you're in bed, well … that's up to you. Be warm, loving and gentle, and you can't go wrong!

Surprise her

Although she is naturally romantic and sensual, she's also moody. Springing something on her if she's not ready will annoy her. If you want to surprise her, make it gradual. Make dinner while she relaxes with a refreshment, let her know a romantic idea you have, give her a sensual backrub – though preferably after dinner, otherwise the food might get cold...!

Spice it up

Use an item that you wouldn't usually bring to bed – something that will stimulate her senses: a warm and aromatic oil, a piece of cashmere to caress her body or a little whipped cream ... keep it sensual.

Remember: She may come across as a kitten, but she is passionate in bed. Her erotic repertoire is impressive, which is the result of her creativity – and her experience.

Her expectations

Sweet suggestions. Don't even think about suggesting anything vulgar; it could put her off sex for weeks. Suggesting a bonk in the copy room at work will seldom go over well (unless, you've really managed to dazzle her).

Sensual setting. When focusing on seducing her, it's important to pay attention to the setting. The female Cancer usually prefers to have sex in the comfort of her own, or her partner's, home. Set the scene with candles, soft music, a glass of wine ... the works.

Keep the lights on. When it comes to the bedroom, she enjoys caressing and fondling her partner's private parts. Don't turn off the lights, because she enjoys admiring them as well.

Frisky and feminine. Although she's not particularly shy, she's rarely sexually aggressive. She may give the man some hints, but she usually prefers him to take control.

Strength and sensuality. She wants a passionate, caring and gentle partner. Touches and caresses should always be soft.

Your sensual preferences
Quiz yourself and find out whether this woman is for you.

Where on the scale are you?
1 = Don't agree | 3 = Sure | 5 = Agree!

1. Caresses and sensual touches are important during sex.
One a scale for 1 to 5, you are: 1 - 2 - 3- 4 - 5

2. Sexual gadgets can be fun, but they're not necessary if the relationship is satisfying.
One a scale for 1 to 5, you are: 1 - 2 - 3- 4 - 5

3. Intimacy and closeness are the basis for a rewarding sex life.
One a scale for 1 to 5, you are: 1 - 2 - 3- 4 - 5

4. Patience is important in the bedroom. Rushing things can ruin the mood.
One a scale for 1 to 5, you are: 1 - 2 - 3- 4 - 5

Score.
15 - 20: Your connection is intense, romantic and very sensual. Enjoy this erotic dream.
10 - 14: The Cancer woman can occasionally be shy. Be patient, guide her gently and let her ease into things.
5 - 9: You probably wish she could be a little less sensitive at times, but it's her nature. Take your time. Enjoy her sensuality.
1 - 4: Either she's too sensitive, or you're too impatient – but you could both benefit from expanding your erotic horizons together.

CHAPTER 4

GENERAL STUFF

The big picture

Keep in mind that the characteristics of a Cancer may vary quite a bit depending on where within the sign she was born, as well as a wide range of additional astrological factors. But for now, let's stick to the basics. Just remember: don't jump to conclusions as soon as you meet her. Give her room to shine. Get to know the woman behind the sign.

Her personality: Pros and cons

Pros	Cons
• Kind	• Sharp-tongued
• Generous	• Moody
• Thoughtful and considerate	• Overly sensitive
• Romantic	• Possessive
• Warm and caring	• Prone to overindulgence
• Soft and feminine	• Argumentative
• Attractive	• Self-pitying
• Affectionate	• Demanding
• Charming and entertaining	• High-maintenance
• Smart	• Emotional
• Sparkling	• Has no tolerance for criticism
• Has an eye for beauty	• Insensitive when provoked
• Idealistic	• Self-obsessed
• Practical and efficient	• A drama queen

Tip: How to show romantic interest

Show romantic attention the old-fashioned way. Try texts, calls, flowers, gifts, dinner invitations … it's all fair game! Make her feel special, but make sure not to overdo it. If you crowd her, she will probably take off.

Romantic Vibes

Miss Cancer:
The romantic and attentive partner

The essence

Either you're in - or not! As soon as she has entered into a relationship, she'll consider you a serious couple. Liberated do-as-you-please partnerships are not her style. If a man feels the need to nurture his free spirit, as far as she's concerned, he can free his spirit somewhere else. She is prepared to make an effort in a relationship, provided her partner shares her enthusiasm.

Romance is everything. Even though she may have short-lived relationships, she seldom refers to them as flings or 'a bit of fun'. Instead, she regards them as little romances. Although she may enjoy a physical fling, love is the fundament that keeps her trying.

Show appreciation. A man will always feel proud to have a Cancer woman by her side. But if she makes an effort to socialise and help him out in social settings, she'll expect him to appreciate her for it later.

Precious attention. Small tokens of affection can make her intensely happy: a loving text message, a rose for no reason, an unexpected gift or some help with something she finds boring. However, when it comes to birthdays or other occasions, she'll expect a nice gift, so you'd better splash out. Something small and sweet will result in an icy stare.

Tip: How to show erotic interest

She can read men like most people read the newspaper. If you're in the mood, a seductive look is usually all it takes to let her know. Add a charming smile, and then look away and allow your interest to sink in.

Erotic Vibrations

Miss Cancer:
The tender and affectionate lover

The essence

Seductress. Although she's undeniably feminine, this woman is no sensitive flower. She can be quite the seductress if she's in the mood – or if she's met a man who dazzles her.

Direct, but subtle. She will never throw herself at a man. She prefers to create sensual sparks by shooting him flirtatious glances. She'll expect him to take it from there. Her hints are gentle, but they're always very direct. A man who doesn't get the message is probably in a coma.

Getting into it. She needs time to loosen up, so don't be impatient. As soon as you have got her in the right mood, she'll prove to be an energetic and engaged lover.

Romantic-erotic flavours. She has the unique ability to combine passion, sensuality and romance: a cocktail that can intoxicate most men. When she finds her man, she will be completely focused on him. The intensity will either scare him off or make him feel like a stud.

In the mood, or moody. She needs to feel intimately and sensually connected to her partner. Don't try seducing her when she's got her mind on other things – or when *you* do. Trying to persuade her to have sex when she's not in the mood will usually end in bad feelings.

CHAPTER 5

COMPATIBILITY QUIZ

Are you banging your head against the wall, or does she unleash your positive potential? Do you provoke her or bring out the best in her? Is she making you throw your arms into the air in exasperation, or do you feel inspired and complete in her company? Take the test to find out.

Question no 1
Do you always tell your woman about your erotic fantasies?

A - Yes, of course I do.
B - My woman is very sensitive, and I try to avoid things that might upset her.
C - Sometimes, but only when I feel they're important to express.

Question no 2
You've been looking forward to a hot and steamy evening. How would you react if your girlfriend lit candles and put on some soft music?

A - I'd love that. I love easing into sensual moods ... it makes everything more intense.
B - Typical. Whenever I want a passionate night, she turns into a soft, cuddly and boring little thing.
C – I might be a little disappointed at first – but I'd be confident that she'd please me by the end of it...

(cont.)

Question no 3
Are you sensitive to your partner's needs?

A - I try, but sometimes I forget – and sometimes, I don't know what she expects from me.
B - Yes. That's very important when you're in a relationship.
C - Only if it will benefit me somehow.

Question no 4
How would you feel if your partner started to sulk after a minor upset?

A – I'd feel annoyed and tell her to pull herself together.
B – I'd leave her alone and give her space until she felt better.
C – I'd talk to her and try to understand her feelings.

Question no 5
How often do you make use of previous experiences with your partner when having sex?

A - I always recall what has previously made my girlfriend happy, and then I build on it.
B - Sometimes I do, sometimes I don't. It depends on the mood.
C - Not really. I usually try to do something new.

Question no 6
You have finally decided to throw out the old jumper you were wearing the first time you met your girlfriend. How would you react when you found it back in your wardrobe the next morning?

A - I'd smile, shrug and leave it there.
B - I'd ask my girlfriend to choose a new jumper for me so we can get rid of this one.
C – I'd throw it away – again!

Question no 7
Do you find it easy to talk about your feelings or any emotional issues?

A – It can be difficult, but I'm willing to try – if I must.
B – Why do feelings have to be involved in every little thing? I hate this 'let's talk' stuff.
C – Yes, I don't have any problems with that.

Question no 8
Be honest: do you enjoy flirting with women other than your partner?

A – Of course. That's what all guys do.
B - I enjoy the attention, but I would never do anything to upset my partner.
C – No, not just for the sake of it. I'm just friendly – with everybody.

Question no 9
Would you say you enjoy the good things in life?

A – Yes: I love good food, a nice atmosphere, close friends and a loving girlfriend…
B – Yes, I enjoy hiking and sleeping outside in my tent. Nice to wake up with the birds.
C – Yes: a fancy car, a nice flat and luxurious holidays are important to me.

Question no 10
Which of the following is an example of something you'd do to please your partner?

A – I'd fix her car or washing machine or something.
B – I'd surprise her with a little gift or a bunch of flowers.
C – I'd take an interest in what she's doing, either her work or hobbies.

SCORE	A	B	C
Question 1	1	10	5
Question 2	10	1	5
Question 3	5	10	1
Question 4	1	5	10
Question 5	10	1	5
Question 6	10	5	1
Question 7	5	1	10
Question 8	1	5	10
Question 9	10	1	5
Question 10	1	10	5

75 – 100

Somehow you know it's right ... it just feels good. Your woman loves your strength and attentiveness, and you embrace her softness, warmth and femininity. You're like two jigsaw pieces, a perfect fit. You are different, but you still seem to match. You're a team, both moving in the same direction. You communicate very well and are sensitive to each other's needs. No silly misunderstandings or upsets here – everything flows effortlessly. This is very promising. Keep inspiring each other...

51 – 74

Apart from a few minor conflicts, this is a pleasant and happy relationship. Togetherness is important to both of you – not only physically, but also mentally. Being on the same level and supporting each other makes everything run smoothly. There's no need to discuss erotic preferences – sensuality is the driving force for both of you. She may be a bit stubborn at times, but remember that there's usually a reason that she puts her foot down – even if you don't agree. She is very sentimental and likes to hold onto what's familiar to her. Don't push her into something new overnight; it will only make her feel uneasy.

26 – 50

'If only she could be a little more [fill in the blank]…' If this comment ever pops up in your mind, it's time to rethink the relationship. You'll either need to accept her as she is or go looking for someone else. An element of adjustment is required for any relationship, but major changes are seldom a good sign. Maybe she feels the same way about you, wishing you would change your ways. Are you prepared to do so? If the distance between you isn't too far, go ahead and figure things out. Try to understand her. Be open and forthcoming. Agree to disagree, and don't freak out about it. If you're both prepared to give a little more of yourselves, this could turn out to be a nice relationship.

10 – 25

Are you smitten with her feminine body and the attention she gives you? Are you captivated by the way she makes you feel like a man? Well, there must be something that keeps you around, because the two of you are very different. It's possible that this relationship is based on a dream. Before you go moving into your castle in the sky – which will probably end in hitting the ground with a bang – you should figure out what you really want. You may discover that the only thing you're good at as a couple is getting on each other's nerves. Save yourself some trouble and be honest with yourself and your partner. Anything is possible, but a harmonious relationship will demand careful attention and hard work.

Thoughts...
If you are too focused on what's visible on the surface, you won't discover love's hidden treasures.

...just a final note:
This book has not been approved by your date and should be treated accordingly. He or she *may* not agree with the content.

www.ingramcontent.com/pod-product-compliance
Lightning Source LLC
Chambersburg PA
CBHW071837020426
42331CB00007B/1768